I feel...

 happy
 calm
 sad
 angry
 worried
 confident

 scared
 surprised
 disgusted
 unsure
 excited
 embarrassed

 panicked
 focused
 disappointed
 silly
 friendly
 jealous

 bored
 muddled
 tired
 unwell
 hungry
 hot or cold

How do I say "I feel angry" in Makaton?

I feel

Take one hand with your thumb pointing upwards and your middle finger pointing to your chest. Bring your hand upwards and say, "I feel".

angry.

With an angry look on your face, claw your hands and make them tense. With palms towards you, move them gently around in front of your chest and say, "angry".

ISBN 978-1-78270-693-9

Copyright © Channon Gray

All rights reserved. No part of this publication may be reproduced or utilised in any form or by any means electronic or mechanical, including photocopying, recording, or by any information storage and retrieval system now known or hereafter invented, without the prior written permission of the publisher and copyright holder.

No part of this book may be used or reproduced in any manner for the purpose of training artificial intelligence technologies or systems. In accordance with Article 4(3) of the DSM Directive 2019/790, Award Publications limited expressly reserves this work from the text and data mining exception.

First published 2026

Published by Award Publications limited
The Old Riding School, Welbeck, Worksop, S80 3LR

awardpublications @award.books
www.awardpublications.co.uk

25-1206 1

Printed in China

All About Angry Scribble

Written and illustrated by
Channon Gray

award

Anger is **tricky.**

It is a feeling that can **grow** quite quickly.

Grr! I am Angry Scribble.

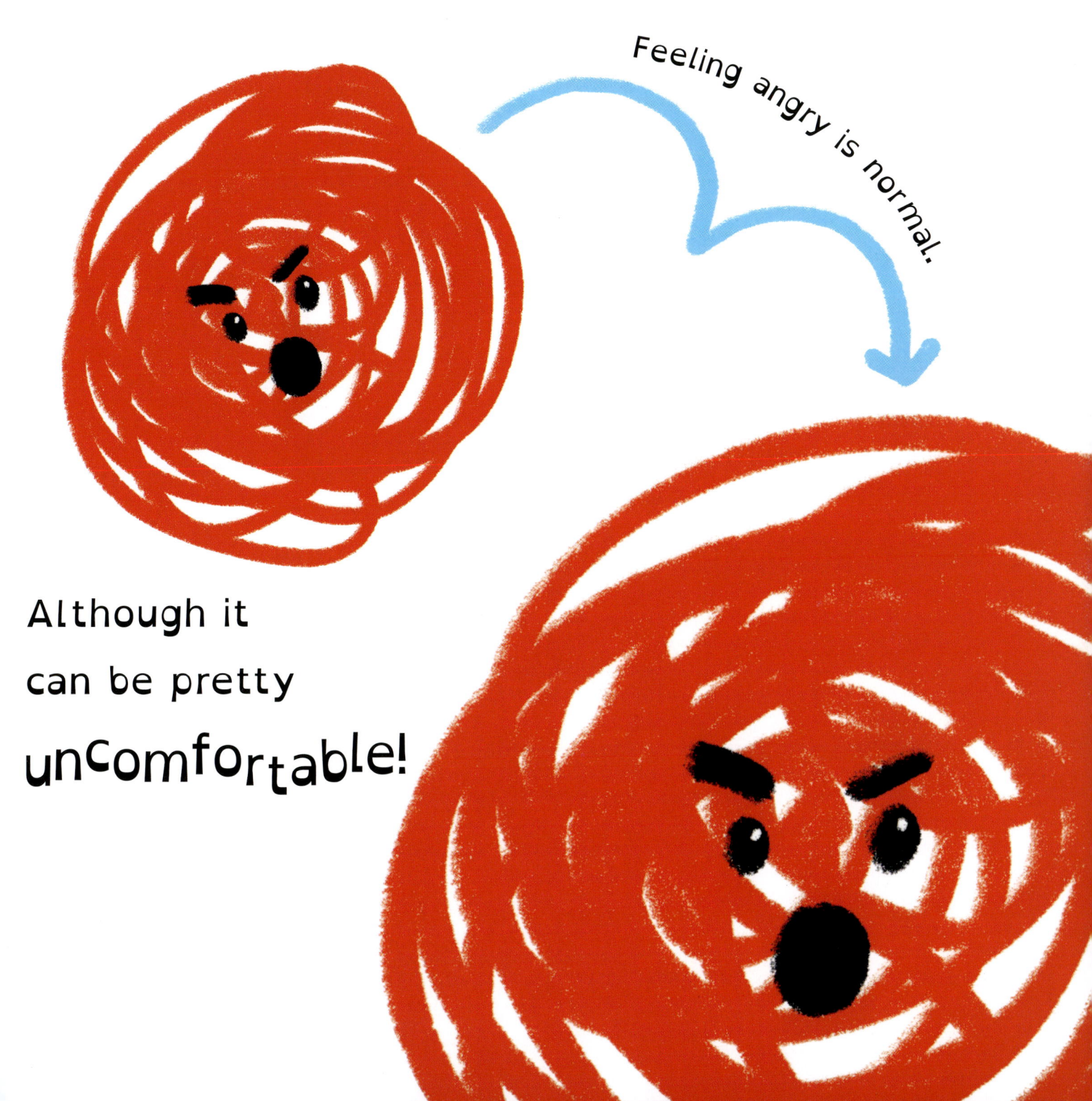

Being tired, hungry or unwell...

...can lead to feeling **aflame.**

Being angry feels and looks different for everyone.

It might make you want to **hit, hide or run.**

It is important to give our feelings, like anger, a name.

Naming our feelings helps them become tame.

Feeling angry can help to keep us safe from danger.

But it can land us in trouble, and be a tricky game-changer.

Anger likes to let us know it is there by making our bodies feel strange things everywhere.

What can you spot?
I am Spot-It Scribble.

Anger can make our

fists clench and our

cheeks turn red.

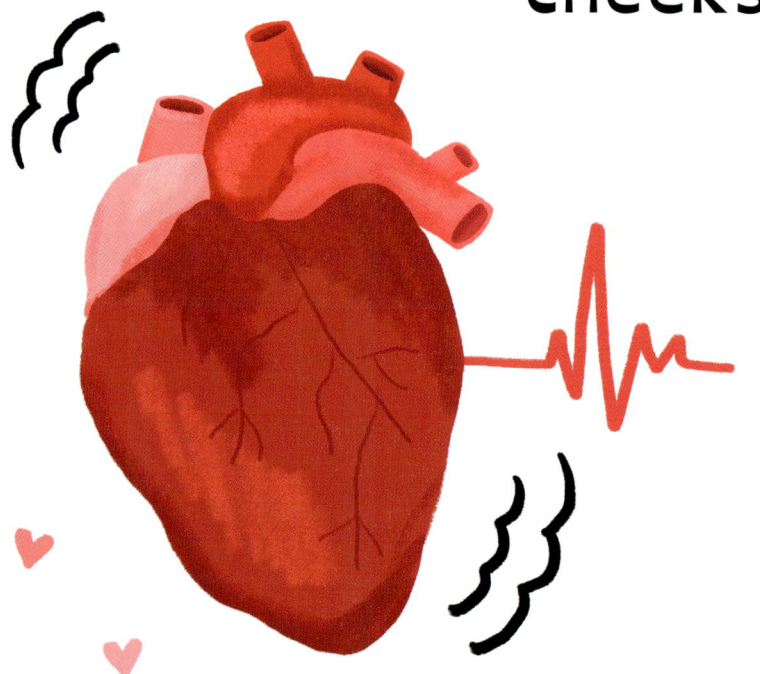

As our heart beats faster, our tummy may begin to fill with rage and with dread.

Anger can make us do things we don't really mean: punch a hole in the wall or let out an angry scream.

We may use our words to hurt others around us, **yell, bite, kick,** break things, or make a BIG fuss!

That's not fair!

AAAAHH!!

"I DON'T CARE!"

Along with anger, other feelings might join in, like sadness or fear.

Eek! I am Scared Scribble.

Sob, sob! I am Sad Scribble.

You may worry no one will listen, no one will hear.

People don't see all the BIG feelings inside you.

Anger may sound **Loud** like **a drill,** or hum quietly like a bee.

the grown-ups who look after me

the weather

the future

what other people do

the news

siblings

I cannot control...

Hmm! I am Focused Scribble.

We are only in control of ourselves.

We cannot control much else.

I can control...

- how I speak to other people
- how I let things affect me
- what I do
- my body boundaries
- when I forgive other people
- how I manage my feelings
- how I treat other people

(not controllable)

- school rules
- how other people manage their feelings
- the past
- the law
- what people think of me
- how other people feel
- friends
- how other people react
- the world
- what other people think

Can you think of any more?

Anger works on a scale.

1 is restful and calm.

Uhh! I am Worried Scribble.

2 and 3 are bubbling and brewing, raising alarm.

4 looks cross and upset.

5 is erupting and exploding with anger.
You are out of control and need to reset!

To feel back in control,
anger needs reminding who is boss.

I can choose my actions!
I am In-Control Scribble.

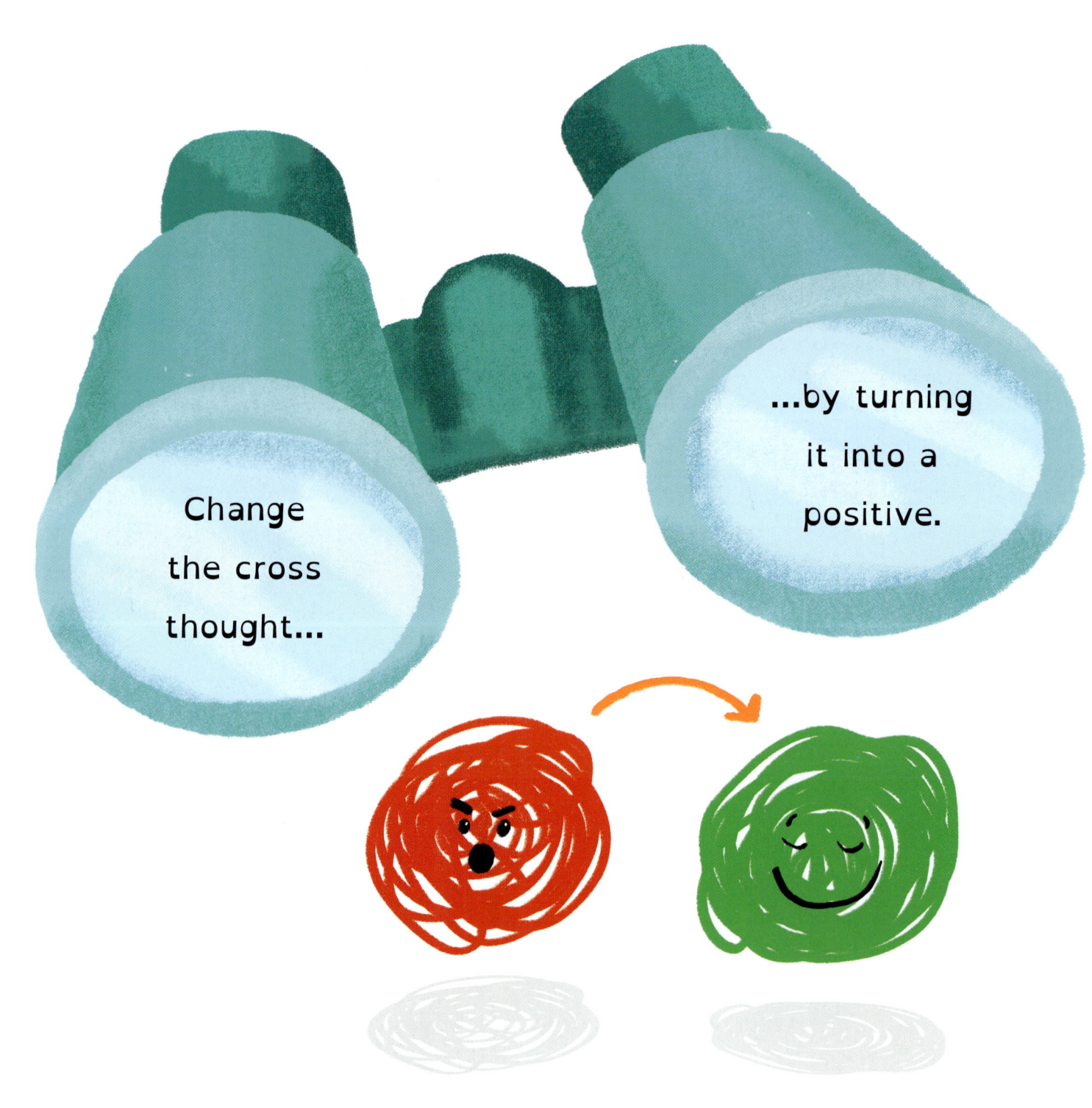

Feelings of anger can bring lots of energy. Move or groove to burn it off!

Or slow down. Squeeze your whole body like a lemon, then let go and brush those angry feelings off.

Your body may feel a little lighter!

Take a deep breath, in through your nose, out through your mouth. Repeat until you feel steady.

Use 5-4-3-2-1. Notice yourself feeling calmer and less edgy.

Use the **5-4-3-2-1** method...

5 things I can see,
4 things I can feel,
3 things I hear,
2 things I can smell,
1 deep breath!

Scribble your feelings to give your mind some space.

Cool yourself down by splashing cold water on your face.

Now you are calm,
you can solve the problem
that made you feel angry.

You may have to be flexible;
it is okay to feel cranky.

Despite what
anger believes,
you are in
control and in
the driving seat.

Angry Scribble Activities

Design your own 'Anger Volcano' to help you to scale your angry feelings.

Create your own 'Anger Toolkit' with strategies to help you to manage your anger in safe and helpful ways.

Get someone to draw around your body on the back of some wallpaper to make your own 'Anger Body Map'.

The Scribbles Crew love to see your creations! Ask your grown-ups to share them on social media using #TheScribblesCrew

Scan the QR code on the back cover for more great Scribbles Crew activities, sing-along songs and teaching resources specially created by The Exciting Teacher.

www.thescribblescrew.com